The Spyders

This book belongs to:

Thompson Nicola Regional Library

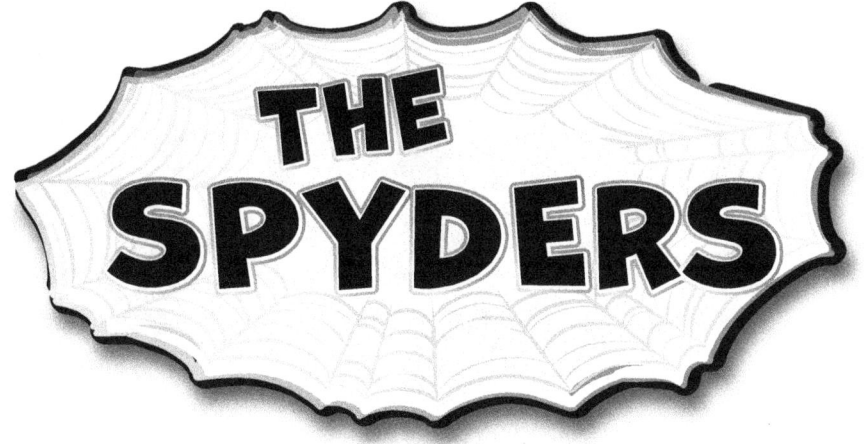

Slither Me Timbers

BOOK #1

Keep Reading!
Vesta Giles

THE SPYDERS
Slither Me Timbers

Vesta L. Giles

Illustrated by
Rebecca McKerchar

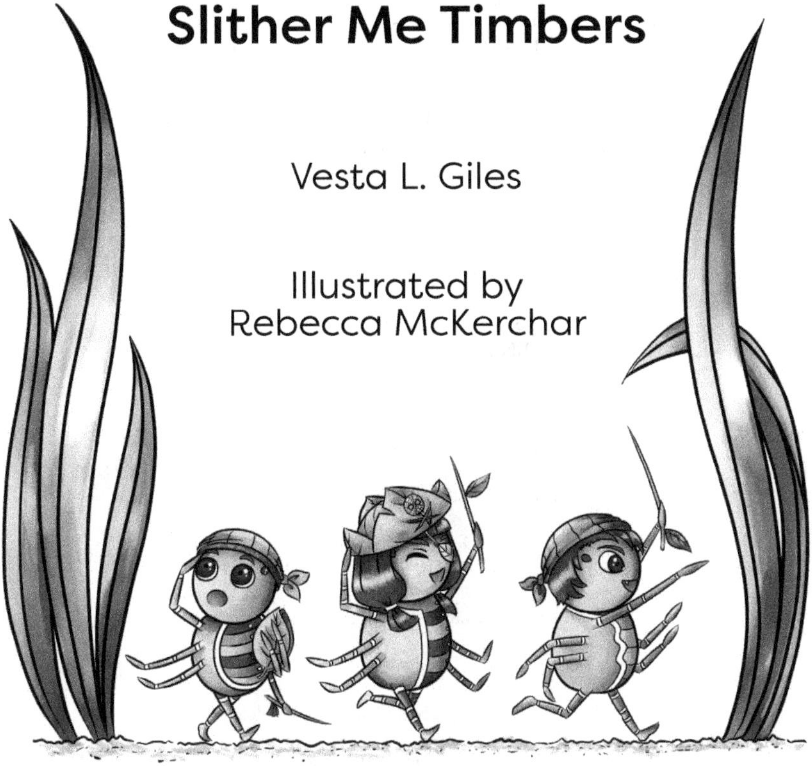

Kamloops, BC, Canada

Thompson Nicola Regional Library
300 - 465 VICTORIA STREET
KAMLOOPS, BC V2C 2A9

The Publisher gratefully acknowledges that they work and live in the Tk'emlúps te Secwépemc territory that is situated in the southern interior of British Columbia within the unceded traditional lands of the Secwepemc Nation. Editing for this book took place in Tofino, BC (Načiks), which is situated on the tip of the Esowista Peninsula, within the traditional Ha-Houthlee (territory) of the Tla-o-qui-aht First Nations and their Tribal Parks. It is bordered, to the north, by the territories of the Ahousaht and Hesquiaht people.

© 2021 by Vesta L. Giles

All rights reserved. This book or parts thereof may not be reproduced in any form, stored in any retrieval system, or transmitted in any form by any means – electronic, mechanical, photocopy, recording, or otherwise – without prior written permission of the publisher.

This is a work of fiction. Any reference to historic events, real people or real places, are used fictitiously. Names, characters, and incidents are products of the author's imagination. Any resemblance to actual people, living or dead, or to any business, event, or locale is purely coincidental.

Issued in print and electronic formats:

ISBN (paperback) 978-1-990353-00-0
ISBN (hardcover) 978-1-990353-03-1
ISBN (epub) 978-1-990353-01-7
ISBN (audio) 978-1-990353-04-8

Illustration: Rebecca McKerchar

Cover Illustration: Rebecca McKerchar

Book Design, Cover Design Layout and Ebook Formatting:
Kristina Benson and Justin Frudd, Dansk Design Group

Editing: Erin Linn McMullan, Fresh Horses

Published in Kamloops, BC, Canada by Vandelso Press

www.vandelsopress.com

*For my mom, Norma,
who inspired a lifetime love
of reading, and is
the best roommate ever!*

Table of Contents

Chapter 1 – Rain, Rain, Go Away 1

Chapter 2 – Pirate Spiders. 17

Chapter 3 – Spiders Ahoy! 30

Chapter 4 – Spiders Overboard! 41

Chapter 5 – Three Spiders and a Snake 50

Chapter 6 – Teamwork 61

Chapter 7 – Cuddles. 67

Chapter 8 – Ready, Aim, Fire! 80

Chapter 9 – Smooth Sailing. 96

Chapter 10 – Flying Spiders. 104

Chapter 11 – Landing 114

Chapter 12 – Spiders Grounded 120

Chapter 1

Rain, Rain, Go Away

The rain just kept falling. Thaddeus Spyder listened to the giant drops hitting the roof over and over again as he did his math homework for the fourth time. It was perfect the first time, but he was bored and there was nothing else to do. Thaddeus had read all the books in the house, twice, and now he was redoing his homework over and over again. And still, it kept raining.

Gracey, Thaddeus's older sister, was busy making sculptures out of webs. Thaddeus watched Gracey build a massive mobile of the solar system. She had been weaving elaborate horses and monsters, and other things out of spider webs for days.

The Spyder family were **Orb-Weaver Spiders** so weaving things out of webs was something they could all do, but Gracey was special. She was an artist, or so she kept reminding Thaddeus and their older brother Curt. Thaddeus could spin a decent web, but he had to work really hard at it, while Curt did only what he needed to pass a test. Gracey, however, was at the top of the advanced web spinning class at school and made sure Thaddeus and Curt never forgot it. Right now, she was really bored too.

Web spinning involved a lot of math and building skills. You had to know how to use the right combination of sticky webs and strong webs. It was required learning for all spiders because it was a survival skill and, well, they were spiders. Making webs is what spiders do.

When it came to survival, though, Curt was an expert. He wasn't really interested in books or art. All he cared about was adventure. He found it impossible to sit still, and his mind was constantly plotting races, and stunts, and things that involved danger. The webs he would spin were meant to help him rappel down from great heights or catapult into the neighbour's yard.

While it rained outside Curt created an obstacle course in the living room with jumps, swings, trampolines, and other things that daredevils loved. He raced through the course over and over to improve his time. Now he tore through his course again. Thaddeus had lost count of how many times he had done it. This time he set a new course speed record.

"Yes!" Curt cried, raising his front legs in triumph. "Two seconds off my best time!"

Unfortunately for Curt, nobody else in the house was paying attention. He'd been running that course over and over for three days.

Of the three Spyder children, Gracey was the tallest, as was often the case with **Orb-Weaver Spiders**. Girls were usually bigger than the boys. Like all of them, she was light reddish brown with white stripes wrapping around her legs. She had long brown hair that she liked to keep in long braids.

Down her back was a long white stripe with delicate points reaching out from it. Curt also had reddish brown legs, but he liked his hair swooping over his eyes because he thought it looked cool, and he had white dots on his back that were all in a straight line. Thaddeus was the smallest, and he liked things to be very precise. His hair was short, and on his back was a white diamond shape. All of them had tiny white bristles resembling hair running up and down their legs. Curt's legs, in particular, were very bristly.

The three Spyder children were so different. They argued a lot, like most brothers and sisters did, but they were still the best of friends. Today, though, after being inside for three whole days, they were just bored.

Martha Spyder, mother of Thaddeus, Gracey, and Curt, was ready for the rain to be over too. She had used up all her rainy-day activity suggestions on the first day of the downpour and now they were on day three. Spyder children cooped up in a house for that many days could only mean one thing…a big mess! She firmly said, "No!" when they begged her to let them build a massive pirate ship in the living room. Thaddeus could tell his mother was impatient by the number of times she rolled her eight eyes whenever they did something. No matter how many eyes they have the mom eye roll is universally understood.

Before the three Spyders went to bed, they all pressed their glum faces against the living room window. The rain was falling in gigantic droplets, running down the window, and making everything outside look dark and blurry.

"Cheer up, you three. The forecast says it's supposed to be sunny tomorrow and that will make all of us happy. Now get ready for bed. Your dad is going to video call in a few minutes to say goodnight."

Harold, father of Thaddeus, Gracey, and

Curt, and husband to Martha, had been away for work and was coming home at the end of the week. Thaddeus couldn't wait. Harold was a spy. Martha was a spy too. Sometimes they worked together and sometimes they worked apart. But they always told the little Spyders about their adventures when they got home from saving the world. Right now, Harold was in a secret location working for the government. Martha was working from home, doing research, handling logistics, and handling their three children. Last week Harold had stayed home with them while she was away working.

When Harold and the children were left unsupervised, they ate a lot of frozen fruit fly pizza. Martha enjoyed cooking more than Harold did. Sometimes he let them stay up too late, but he still made them do all of their chores. And when Martha was on her way home, they cleaned like mad spiders.

Sometimes, when both of their parents were away working, their grandparents or their Aunt Octavia stayed with them. Those were fun times but they still had to wash their faces, brush their fangs, and do their homework.

The Spyder house was small and tucked in next to the human house near their front door. It was quaint in the style of an English spider cottage with white walls and a happy red door. They had their own little garden where the Spyder kids, and their dad, loved to play.

Before they went to bed each of the Spyders had to gather all the webs they made during the day. Then they sat down at the kitchen table and ate them. It's what spiders do. It helped them refill their silk storage and it replaced some of the energy they lost making webs, which was really hard work. Curt, more than almost anything else, hated eating his webs.

> **Spider Fact:** Spiders really do eat their webs at the end of the day. It helps them replace the silk they used up making webs all day, and it gives them energy.

"It's so gross!" he complained, just like he did every night. "Why do we have to do this?"

"Curt," their mother replied as she placed her own webs on a plate and sat at the table. "You've been a spider your whole life, it shouldn't be a surprise to you that you have to eat your webs. And like it or not, you're still going to have to do it tomorrow night, and every other night."

Thaddeus couldn't blame him. Curt's webs were always limp and covered in dirt and other disgusting things. Gracey also hated eating her webs. She didn't like it because it meant ruining her masterpieces. Every once in awhile she was allowed to keep one, or one was submitted for an art exhibition, but in the end, she still had to eat most of them, even the most beautiful. Tonight, their mother let her keep her solar system up because Gracey insisted it wasn't finished yet. She still needed to eat the others, though. She looked crushed. Thaddeus, however, didn't mind eating his webs although he preferred his with a little bit of ketchup.

After their video chat with their father, the three Spyder children climbed into their separate sleeping pods. Each pod hung from the ceiling of their bedroom. Thaddeus's pod had pictures of great scientists stuck to his walls, and stacks of books everywhere. He loved his pod and loved to sit there and read or write stories or draw. Gracey's pod, slightly above the one Thaddeus had, was full of drawings for her sculptures and posters of great art. Curt's pod, at the top, was a mess. He was only ever in it when he was sleeping. It had posters of daredevils and superheroes all over the walls and broken sports equipment everywhere.

Right before bed they all read for awhile. Curt read books about adventurers. Thaddeus fell asleep with *Advanced Arachnid Physics* while Gracey pored over her tattered copy of *Modern Web Sculpture* with a flashlight after they were supposed to have the lights out. Soon they were all curled up in their pods, fast asleep.

The next morning, Thaddeus, as usual, was the first to get up. He climbed out of his pod, his eyes still not fully open, and promptly tripped over Gracey's solar system sculpture. The sticky webs stuck to the bristles on his legs. He spun around and was instantly covered in a sticky intergalactic mess. Jupiter and Saturn merged, and Mars hit him square on the head. The planets were destroyed. Walking backwards into the living room he tried to free himself from the webs that were now wrapped all around him. He started to fall and landed on the trampoline that Curt had strung between the sofa and the coffee table. From the trampoline, Thaddeus bounced straight toward the window where he stuck, upside down, with no hope of escape on his own.

Firmly cemented to the window, the littlest spider took note of his surroundings. He was completely stuck and couldn't move a muscle. He could, however, see out the window. What he saw made him happier than he had been in days. The sun! Thaddeus saw the sun shining brightly through the window, lighting up the garden, and sparkling off the webs that were holding him captive.

"The sun is shining!" he exclaimed.

Sleepily, Gracey and Curt made their way out of the bedroom.

"What happened to my solar system?" Gracey called with dismay.

Martha, who was walking down the hallway in her robe, casually dodged the destroyed planets and walked into the living room. "Darling, you can make another one and you should know better than to leave your projects lying around. I think the more important question is, 'What happened to our Thaddeus?'"

The three of them surveyed the damage

and assessed the plight of Thaddeus.

"A little help, please?" he asked.

"You two help get Thaddeus down," said Martha. "I'll start breakfast. It will be good for all of you to get outside."

Chapter 2

Pirate Spiders

With their bellies full of fruit fly porridge, the three little Spyders set out for an adventure in the sunshine.

They could hear their mother's voice ringing in their ears. "Don't go too far," she told them, and "stay away from the puddle!" Then she had given them that look that moms all have when they really want to make sure you're listening – the "mom" look that only moms can do.

It was a beautiful day, and they were free!

The air smelled sweet after the rain and the sunshine felt good on their faces. Curt, Gracey, and Thaddeus ran and played together all morning. Curt swung through the branches of a shrub on webs he spun himself. They broke, of course, but Curt didn't care. Gracey darted back and forth, weaving beautiful designs that sparkled with droplets of water she captured, leftovers from the rain. Thaddeus cartwheeled and squealed with glee. The three stretched their 24 combined legs that had been cooped up for far too long. It was a glorious morning! They raced past the gigantic downspout that all spiders are warned to stay away from, and then played on some toys left outside by the kids in the big house. They climbed on the abandoned toy tractor, one of their favourite things in the yard, and then they made swings out of webs and hung them from the handlebars of the old, rusted tricycle that had been there forever.

Curt led the way into a small forest of shrubs. Before long the three emerged into a small clearing. Curt and Gracey froze. Thaddeus cartwheeled right into them. All three stared at the most amazing sight that was right before them – the puddle, bigger than they had ever seen it. Waves were lapping gently against the shore. A gigantic dish-shaped leaf floated in the shallow water.

Thaddeus closed all eight of his eyes and he could just see his mother's face in front of him giving him the mom look. Her voice echoed in his ears, "Don't go near the water!"

"Whoa," said Curt, looking in awe at the leaf.

"I think we went too far from the house," Gracey said.

"We're not supposed to be at the puddle!" moaned Thaddeus.

As if he hadn't heard his brother or sister, Curt just kept looking up at the floating leaf. It was perfect. There were no holes and the sides rose up very high. Thaddeus looked over at him and was sure he could actually see Curt's brain working. Curt was looking at the leaf, and Thaddeus knew what was coming. He looked at Gracey and saw her glazed expression. He knew they were thinking the same thing. He also knew his brother and sister were highly skilled at ignoring their mother's warnings when they saw something tempting. It was like the leaf was just waiting for them. Even Thaddeus saw the potential. This leaf, they all knew, was the perfect pirate ship!

The bristles on all eight of Thaddeus's legs stood to attention. This, he recognized, was the first sign of danger.

"Hey," Thaddeus cautioned, "remember Mom told us not to go too far away and we are really far from the house!"

"Define 'too far'?" countered Curt.

Gracey, who was already lost in thought,

designing the most amazing pirate ship sails spider-kind had ever seen, agreed.

"He's right. She didn't say how far was too far."

"Well, she definitely told us not to go near the puddle," Thaddeus pointed out.

"We didn't go looking for the puddle," Curt said as he began gathering twigs and leaves. "We found it by accident, and it's a lot closer to the house than it normally is."

Thaddeus rolled all of his eyes. *Here we go again*, he thought. *We're going to be grounded and doing extra chores for sure. That is, of course, if we survive Curt's questionable construction methods.*

Spider Fact: Most spiders have eight eyes, but their eyes don't move around like human eyes do. They are fixed. The front eyes are used for hunting and the side eyes detect motion, which can save them from predators.

As if Curt could hear what Thaddeus was thinking, he stopped and looked directly at his younger brother.

"Thad," he said. "How often do we get to be real pirates? We'll just go out a little ways and then come back. What could go wrong?"

What could go wrong? the thought bounced around Thaddeus's brain. He and Gracey looked at each other with a "Remember the last time he said that?" look. Thaddeus looked at Gracey. Gracey looked at Thaddeus. All three of them looked at the boat. Thaddeus knew even he couldn't resist.

But Thaddeus was not as brave as his older brother and he suspected how this was going to end. Even though spiders and water were a bad combination, Curt and Gracey were still good swimmers when they had to be. Thaddeus, however, was not. Instead of helping with the construction of the boat, he made his way back into the forest for an important project of his own.

Later, Thaddeus heard Curt calling, "Thad, where are you? We're ready to set sail!"

"Just a minute," Thaddeus called from the forest.

Moments later, Thaddeus emerged from the forest wearing an expertly made life jacket. It was constructed out of leaves which had been sewn together into tube shapes with fine webbing. The tubes had then been inflated to make a perfectly fitting life jacket guaranteed to keep any little spider afloat, no matter what happened. There was no way Thaddeus was going down with any ship.

"Don't you trust us?" Gracey asked,

"Who built the boat?" Thaddeus asked as he stared pointedly at her.

Curt and Gracey looked each other, a little unsure.

"We did."

"Exactly. Your track record in the field of construction isn't the greatest."

Curt, in particular, was offended. "Hey, that tree house collapsed because of termites!"

"Right," said Thaddeus in mock agreement. Even Gracey was looking a little unsure.

Then Thaddeus looked past Curt and Gracey and realized they were standing in front of the coolest pirate ship he had ever seen.

The hull was made of the green leaf. It had a deck made from twigs that had been lashed together, packed with mud, and attached to the hull so the leaf would keep its shape. It had beautiful sails with skulls and crossbones woven into the design. In the back was a rudder made of a narrow triangular leaf lashed to a twig.

"Wow," Thaddeus exclaimed. "Nice job on the sails, Gracey!"

Gracey beamed.

On the side of the ship was painted the name, *Arachnia*. Thaddeus's heart pounded with excitement. This was a real pirate ship!

The *Arachnia* floated near the edge of the shore and appeared, from Thaddeus's perspective, to be seaworthy. A rope ladder hung down the side, waiting for them to come aboard.

Curt and Thaddeus stepped forward before Gracey called, "Wait!"

They turned to look and saw that their sister was wearing a pirate hat. She had an eye patch made out of leaves that covered her front left eye. She held a hat and a patch out to each of her brothers. Curt found a small piece of feather and stuck it in his hat. It looked perfect! Once they put them on, Gracey handed them peg legs – tubes made from leaves that went over top of their real leg, and swords made out of webbing and twigs.

"Cool!" the brothers exclaimed together. Curt held up his sword and stabbed at the air in a classic sword fighting stance. He actually felt like a pirate. He was suddenly walking and talking like a real pirate! Thaddeus, a little wobbly on his peg leg, felt the same.

The three siblings in their pirate gear grinned at each other. All at once their swords were raised, the tips pointing together, and they all yelled, "Arrr!" at the same time. They burst out laughing and scrambled up the ladder to the deck of their very own pirate ship, thankful they had seven other legs to make up for their peg leg. Climbing a ladder with a peg leg was not as easy as they thought it would be.

Chapter 3

Spiders Ahoy!

The cool fresh sea air was pounding Thaddeus in the face while Curt and Gracey pounded each other with swords a few feet behind him. There was nothing like playing pirate on an actual pirate ship! Thaddeus stood at the bow of the ship looking in amazement at the shoreline flying by. They had caught a gentle breeze and the sails of the *Arachnia* were full, propelling them to destinations unknown.

Curt and Gracey turned and realized Thaddeus wasn't part of the sword fighting action. They soon fixed that with a well-timed ambush. Thaddeus wobbled on his peg leg and his pirate hat fell over his eyes, but he managed to keep his sword up. Soon he was sword fighting his way across the deck. The three of them were locked in a battle on their own pirate ship. This was the best day ever!

Curt, Gracey, and Thaddeus tumbled across the *Arachnia*'s deck – like one hairy brown mass locked together with legs flying in every direction. Laughing, they broke apart and collapsed on the deck, out of breath.

"I love being a pirate spider!" Curt cried with joy.

"Well, you know we're not *real* **Pirate Spiders**, right?" said Gracey.

"Oh yeah, she's right. That would not be a good thing!" Thaddeus agreed.

"Why?" asked Curt as he stood up and dusted himself off.

"Because real **Pirate Spiders** eat other spiders! Didn't you pay attention in school?" Gracey exclaimed.

Curt looked at her, shocked. "You mean there are spiders that eat other spiders?"

"Yes!" Thaddeus and Gracey answered together.

"Yuck!" was Curt's reply as Gracey and Thaddeus got up.

> **Spider Fact:** Pirate Spiders really do eat other spiders. They are found all over the world but the highest numbers are in Central and South America.

Curt jumped into a sword fighting stance and lunged at Gracey.

"Arrr!" cried Curt as he thrust his pretend sword that was really a twig.

Thaddeus's hat fell over his eyes again.

"Don't Arrr me, matey! I'll swab the deck with ye and use your eight hairy legs to clean my cannons!" Gracey lunged back.

Thaddeus managed to straighten his hat and pushed his sword toward Curt. "Avast ye scoundrels!" Thaddeus cried.

Curt stopped and stood up, forgetting his pirate stance.

"Wait! You'll what?" he said to Gracey.

Gracey, not abandoning her pirate character, repeated. "I'll clean my cannons with your hairy legs!"

"That's disgusting," Curt scowled.

Pouncing on Curt's confusion and disgust, Gracey and Thaddeus attacked.

"Arrr!" they cried together, backing Curt against the side of the ship with their swords.

Later, exhausted from sword fighting, the three Spyder pirates were grinning with their faces in the breeze as the *Arachnia* sailed the high seas of the mud puddle in the garden. The shoreline was a blur of rocks, weeds, and abandoned toys from the human children. In the distance they could see the human house looming over the entire garden.

Curt scanned the horizon with a spy glass from a crow's nest perched precariously high up on the main mast. Far down below, Gracey was at the helm and Thaddeus, secure in his life jacket, stood at the bow with the cold wind rushing through the bristles on his eight legs. He gripped the sides of the ship with four of his legs and fought to stand up in the wind.

In the far distance Thaddeus could see an old red-and-white tennis shoe abandoned on its side in the puddle. He knew it belonged to one of the human children. They were constantly leaving their things laying about in the yard. Curt, from high above, saw it too.

"Land ahead! We'll round the 'Shoe of Terror' and it should be clear sailing past the 'Island of Doom'! We'll be home in plenty of time for dinner!" Curt called out.

"Aye, aye, Captain Hairy Legs!" Gracey called back. Thaddeus giggled.

Thaddeus saw the island near the shoe. He didn't know why Curt called it the Island of Doom. It didn't look that scary. He shrugged and kept enjoying the wind.

Curt hung onto the mast with one leg. He looked through the spotting scope, which was really a rolled-up leaf with a droplet of water at the end, and surveyed the scene before him. The wind had increased, and they were approaching the shoe at great speed.

No problem, Curt thought to himself. *The Arachnia can make that corner at this speed. It's totally doable.* He saw the island approaching quickly. He gulped.

"Ahoy matey, thar be land ahead! Hard to port so we don't run aground!" Curt called to Gracey from up above. The *Arachnia* strained as Gracey made the hard turn.

Thaddeus looked down at the deck below his feet. One of the web ropes holding the deck together snapped as he watched. Seeing water sloshing below him told him that the leaf that made up the hull had a hole in it. Swiftly moving water could be seen be seen in the newly formed gap. Thaddeus tightened his life jacket.

"Uh, Captain Hairy Legs? You might want to see this!" he called out. Nobody was listening.

"The wheel is stuck!" cried Gracey. Both Thaddeus and Curt turned to look at their sister. Gracey had all of her legs braced against anything she could find, trying to turn the wheel which wouldn't budge.

Curt started climbing down the mast but before he could reach the deck the *Arachnia* lurched sideways.

Thaddeus looked down in alarm as the webs tying the deck pieces together began to pop one by one. The deck was what kept the hull from flopping open.

Gracey was pushing as hard as she could

on the wheel when it suddenly let go. She fell backwards and the wheel started spinning out of control. The ship lurched the other way. Gracey was thrown across the deck while Curt dangled from the mast, unable to get the rest of his legs to grasp the pole. Thaddeus, in the meantime, was thrown facedown on the deck, or what was left of the deck. He looked down and saw only water below. The leaf that had made up the hull of the boat was gone!

"I think you should see this!" he yelled in panic.

Suddenly a wave reached up above them and crashed down onto the deck. The *Arachnia* disintegrated beneath them, sending debris and three little spiders into the cold dark water.

Chapter 4

Spiders Overboard!

Spiders and water are not a good combination. Some spiders can swim, but in general, spiders don't like water.

Gracey opened her eyes and looked around. She was bobbing up and down in the puddle. Pieces of the *Arachnia*, some large and some very small, were floating all around her. Keeping her head above the water, she swam over to a nearby piece of the deck and wrapped one of her soggy legs around it. She was exhausted and well and truly waterlogged. With her last bit of energy, she heaved her body onto a piece of the deck, her legs flopping in a lifeless pile. Finally able to rest, she took a deep breath and stared at the blue sky above her. It was then that she remembered where she was and everything that had happened. Her heart wrenched in terror.

Spider Fact: Most spiders can't swim but there are some that can walk on water and others that walk underwater, crawling over rocks. Some even hunt and eat small fish!

"Thaddeus! Curt! Where are you?" she called out, panicking. *Oh, Mom is going to be really mad if we let something happen to Thaddeus,* she thought to herself.

From a distance she heard what sounded like a small motor. She searched the debris for its source. To her relief, she saw Thaddeus, perfectly safe in his life jacket, racing toward her using several of his legs like propellors. He was a regular motorboat and looked perfectly fine.

"Gracey! I was looking everywhere! Are you OK? Where's Curt?" he asked, so relieved to see her.

"I'm OK," she answered. "I don't know where Curt is!"

From the other side of a large piece of the *Arachnia*'s hull hey heard a gargling groan.

"Ow!" Curt moaned.

"Curt!" Gracey called. "Where are you? Are you OK?"

Gracey grabbed onto Thaddeus and helped kick as he spider-backed her to where Curt was floating. He was a long way away and looked like a floating mass of hairy legs.

Gracey spun a superstrong web and wound it like a lasso above her head. "Curt, grab this!"

From the middle of the floating pile of Curt, an eye opened. Curt looked over toward his brother and sister. Gracey spun the lasso once, twice, and then on the third time let go. Thanks to Gracey's outstanding throwing arm, the web rope easily made it. Curt thrust one of his legs up in the air just in time to grab the rope as it sailed over his head.

"Hold on!" Gracey yelled.

Thaddeus turned around and with Gracey's help, propelled all three of them toward the shore of the tiny island in the middle of the puddle.

A little while later, the three little spiders were dragging themselves out of the water and onto the island. The three stood onshore, dripping dry while they surveyed what was left of the ship.

"Well," Curt said, as he picked up the part of the hull with the name *Arachnia* painted on it, "it could be worse."

"Uh, we're stuck on an island with no way home and if we ever do make it home Mom is going to ground us for life for doing what she specifically told us not to do," Thaddeus pointed out.

"And she was right," Gracey said glumly as she kicked a piece of what had once been the steering wheel. "We can deal with mom later. Let's figure out a way to get home," Curt said optimistically as he faced the water and looked for options. For Curt, there were always options. It's just that sometimes, his options weren't very good. "And really, what else could possibly go wrong? It's not like there are snakes or anything. Look at the bright side!"

Thaddeus felt the hairs on the back of his neck rise in warning just as a huge shadow moved over him from behind. The shadow was long, and tall, and appeared to have a…head!

"Uh, Curt," Thaddeus said in a very small voice. "I hate to rain on your parade but…."

Curt turned around to face Thaddeus and froze. His eyes grew enormous. He shook in terror as he looked past Thaddeus and Gracey.

Thaddeus turned around just in time to see the scaly yellow belly of a young snake towering over top of them. The snake, a common Garter Snake, looked equally horrified and its eyes were huge.

Curt and the snake yelled at the same time:
"Snake!"   "Spiders!"

Then the tall snake, and the little spider, both rolled their eyes and promptly fainted right there on the spot.

Thaddeus and Gracey each dove to one side to avoid being squashed by the snake's gigantic wobbling head.

Curt landed with a thud and the snake landed with a bigger thud. The spider and the snake were right next to each other. Had they both been conscious, they would have been staring at each other eye to eye.

Thaddeus and Gracey stood up, dusted themselves off, and stared down at the peaceful faces of Curt and the snake.

"It had to be snakes," Gracey said as she looked admiringly at the black-and-red patterning and the long yellow stripe down the back of the snake.

"Yup," Thaddeus agreed. "The one thing in the whole world Curt is afraid of. Now he is right, it can't get any worse."

Chapter 5

Three Spiders and a Snake

Curt and the snake both began to regain consciousness at about the same time and they both jumped to their feet. Actually, the snake didn't have feet but it jumped to its coils.

Bracing themselves, Thaddeus and Gracey stood shoulder to shoulder, facing the snake as it rose up and up and up to stand as tall as it could above them. Gracey was sure it was even taller than it had been before, and its huge dark eyes were staring down at them in a menacing glare. Now that the shock of seeing a snake had worn off, Gracey and Thaddeus both noticed that the snake had an eye patch similar to theirs, so really, only one eye was glaring. Curt, now cowering behind them, was too scared to notice. All he could see was a snake, and Curt was deathly afraid of snakes.

Gracey looked more closely at the snake.

"I think it's still a baby," she whispered to Thaddeus.

"I think it's scared of us," he whispered back.

Curt, hearing this discussion, couldn't stand it anymore.

"Scared? Of us? Why would an evil spider-eating snake be scared of us?"

The snake reared up even taller and looked a little insulted. It obviously heard Curt. In an instant it went from frightened to offended.

"Evil? Who are you calling evil? You're creepy poisonous spiders with seven too many legs!" it snorted.

Now it was Gracey's turn to be offended.

"Hey! Hold on! We're not poisonous! We're **Orb-Weaver Spiders**. Get your species straight, buster!"

The snake was taken aback, and then immediately Gracey realized it felt bad. He hung his head.

"I'm sorry. I've never actually talked to spiders before," said the snake.

"Thank you," Gracey replied. She turned to Curt. "And you've never actually talked to a snake before, right?"

Curt looked up, trying to not make eye contact with his sister.

"And I'm pretty sure," she continued, "if this snake was going to eat us it would have already done it!"

Curt still looked resistant. Gracey stared at him, locking him in her steely gaze.

"Yeah," he finally relented. "I guess. I'm sorry too."

"Great, now that we're all going to get along, I'm Gracey." She pointed to Thaddeus, "This is my younger brother, Thaddeus."

Thaddeus waved several of his legs at the snake.

"And this," Gracey continued, pointing at Curt, "is our older brother, Curt."

Curt, still wary, offered a half-hearted wave.

"Hi, I'm Alvin!" The snake brightened and gave them his best smile.

The four grinned, knowing they had now become friends, even if Curt was still a little wary.

"Are you pirates?" Alvin asked, "I love playing pirates."

Thaddeus surveyed the debris of the *Arachnia* floating near the shore.

"We were," he answered, "but we just got shipwrecked and I don't know if we'll even get home. Plus, our mom told us not to go near the water and now we're going to be in sooooo much trouble!"

"The *Arachnia* is definitely toast," admitted Curt.

"And so are we," Gracey agreed.

"I was playing pirates too and I got lost," the snake said sadly. "The grass is too tall, and I can't find my way home."

Curt warmed a little to his new friend. "So," he asked, "you're really not going to eat us, right?"

Alvin gagged a little and gave a shiver. "Ew! Our family doesn't eat spiders, except for the occasional black widow."

Curt looked appreciatively at Alvin. "Well,

that's OK then. So, you're a snake who is scared of spiders?"

"And you're a spider who is scared of snakes?"

Thaddeus rolled his eyes one by one as he saw the two one-time enemies become strange friends. But he had bigger things to think about, like how they were going to get home.

Alvin lowered his head and stared straight at Curt, pondering his new friend. Curt stretched his head as far as he dared toward Alvin. They stared at each other, checking each other out eye to eye, eye patch to eye patch.

"Can I interrupt your staring contest?" asked Thaddeus.

Reluctantly, both Alvin and Curt broke their stare down and turned to look at

Thaddeus.

"We need to get home before dinner and Alvin wants to get to his home too. Maybe we can help each other."

Gracey understood where Thaddeus was going with this. They were going to need to work as a team.

"If we're going to be a pirate crew, we're going to need to get a hat and a peg for your tail, Alvin," she decided.

She looked straight at Alvin and raised her one leg like a sword. "Arrr!" she cried.

"Arrr!" Thaddeus raised his arm toward Gracey's.

"Arrr!" Curt's leg shot up in agreement.

Alvin proudly raised the tip of his tail to meet

the raised legs of his new friends. "Arrr!" he shouted happily.

Under Gracey's direction, they all got to work gathering whatever materials they could find.

A short time later, Alvin and the three little spiders all gazed in admiration at Alvin's reflection in the calm water. The snake wore a fine-looking pirate hat and peg tail that Gracey had fashioned for him out of the wreckage of the *Arachnia*.

Alvin was beyond thrilled. It was the first, and best pirate hat he had ever worn.

"Well, slither me timbers!" he cried. "Look at me! Now I really look like a pirate!"

He joyously gave a little flick of his peg tail.

Meanwhile, Thaddeus was eyeing some triangular leaves on the shore. A plan was beginning to form in his mind. He picked up the leaves and inspected them closely. He held up one of his legs and carefully watched as the bristles moved gently in the breeze.

Thaddeus did some quick calculations using a stick in the dirt and began drawing some detailed plans. Gracey looked over his shoulder.

"I see where you're going with that," she nodded. "Yeah, that should work."

Curt and Alvin looked too.

"I don't get it," Curt said, puzzled. He angled his head to see if it made any more sense sideways.

Alvin also looked confused and turned his head the other way as he looked at the plans. Nope, it didn't make any sense to him either.

Thaddeus kept drawing.

> **Spider Fact:** While some insects like ants have three main body segments, spiders only have two. And spiders have eight legs while most other insects have six.

Chapter 6

Teamwork

Curt adjusted the harness that was now strapped around his chest and shoulders. He pulled his helmet, made of a nutshell, firmly down ontop of his pirate hat.

"This is awesome, Thad!" Curt called, grinning from ear to ear.

Gracey, also in a harness and helmet, was less excited. She adjusted the harness for the hundredth time. Then she gave a hard tug to the long line of web connecting her to a similar harness wrapped around Alvin's tail. She and Curt were both securely tethered to Alvin.

"I'm not convinced about this," she said. "Are you sure it's safe?" She looked back at the large kite-shaped leaf attached to her back.

Thaddeus put his own helmet on and looked back at Curt and Gracey with their matching helmets, harnesses, and kites.

"Nothing to worry about, Gracey," he called back to her. "It's my math and your webs so it should be perfectly safe. Curt had nothing to do with it!"

Spider Fact: Spiders spin webs using organs on their abdomen called spinnerets. They can create up to seven different kinds of web strands depending on what they need.

"Hey!" Curt protested.

Alvin waited patiently as Thaddeus climbed up his neck. And then he looked back, alarmed, as Thaddeus slid right back down and landed with a thump.

"Ow! Uh, Alvin?"

Alvin looked down at the tiny spider.

"Yeah?"

"Do you mind if I sit on your hat? I can't find anything to hold onto."

"Arrr!" Alvin proclaimed, as he bent his head low to the ground. Thaddeus climbed aboard and nestled himself into the dip in the top of Alvin's pirate hat.

Once Thaddeus was settled in, he and Alvin looked back at Curt and Gracey.

"Ready for takeoff?" Alvin called to them.

"Ready!" Curt had a huge smile stuck on his face.

Gracey looked much less convinced.

"Sure," she answered, sounding anything but sure.

"We live on the other side of the garden shed," said Alvin, "in a clearing with some big rocks. The grass and shrubs are too thick for me to see."

"Don't worry, Alvin!" Curt called from behind them. "We'll find it!"

"Arrr!" The four friends cried their pirate battle cry together. Alvin slowly began to slither through the water remembering to keep his tail pointing straight up. The web lines connecting Gracey and Curt to Alvin tightened as he picked up speed. The webs tugged and suddenly Curt and Gracey were lifted high, flying above Alvin and Thaddeus. They were paragliding in harnesses and kites that held firm thanks to Thaddeus's exceptional knowledge of physics and Gracey's unparalleled web-spinning skills.

Curt and Gracey, her pigtails sailing behind her, soared high above the puddle looking down over the garden world of the three spiders and their new snake friend.

"Woohoo!" Curt yelled as the wind whipped at his face.

Chapter 7

Cuddles

Flying behind Alvin, Curt was in his glory. This was the best day ever! He looked over at Gracey. Her eyes were squeezed shut. He knew she hated heights.

"Gracey," he nudged. "It's OK. You can open your eyes! It's amazing!"

Finding her courage, Gracey opened her eyes and saw Curt grinning. She looked down and caught her breath. She was scared, but it was so beautiful. Her heart was in her throat, but she really was OK.

The garden looked so cool from their new perspective. As Curt and Gracey soared up high, they marvelled at how different things looked from above.

There was the puddle far below them and what could be seen of the wreckage of the *Arachnia*, and there was the Shoe of Terror. The world looked smaller from up high but there was so much more of it than Curt had ever known.

When Curt saw they were approaching the garden shed he also realized with a start what time it was. There was always a danger in the area of the shed in the afternoons.

"Hey Alvin," Curt called down. "Hard to starboard! Steer clear of the garden shed. We don't want to run into...."

Alvin heard Curt but knew it was too late to slow down. He and Thaddeus were already rounding the corner when they came to a sudden and screeching stop. Thaddeus's legs were scrambling in all directions trying to find something to grab onto while his body kept hurtling forward. He tumbled down off Alvin's pirate hat, over Alvin's snout, and landed in an undignified heap on the ground.

As soon as Alvin stopped moving forward Curt and Gracey fell from the sky in a pile of twisted bits of web, kites, and spider legs.

Curt got up first and dusted himself off. He helped Gracey up.

"You OK?" he asked.

"Ow!" Gracey replied. "Yeah, I'm OK. You?"

"I'm good, but we've got to run!"

Curt grabbed one of Gracey's legs and they raced around the corner of the shed where they faced their biggest fear. There were Alvin and Thaddeus, both rooted to the ground, frozen in terror. Facing them, his lips pulled back in an evil grin that showed off a mouth full of sharp dagger-like teeth, was the mortal enemy of almost every creature that lived in the garden.

"Cuddles," Curt groaned under his breath.

"Oh no," whispered Gracey.

Cuddles was a gigantic orange tabby cat who lived in the main house. He had long hair that made him look bigger and scarier than he really was. Every summer his humans gave him a haircut that left most of his body, except his head, nearly bald. The result was a small, nearly hairless body attached to a gigantic fluffy orange head. A terror to all creatures that were smaller than him, he hated the spiders more than anything.

All the creatures in the garden knew it was haircut time for Cuddles because, while he was always mean, his haircut put him in a really bad mood. Cuddles, the spiders and Alvin all noticed, had just had his haircut. This was not a good sign.

Forgetting he was still in his harness, Curt ran to grab Thaddeus and pull him out of the way. The webbing that had previously connected him to Alvin was caught on a rosebush. Curt ran as hard as he could and realized too late what was happening.

"Curt, stop!" Gracey called, but he didn't hear.

The web stretched and stretched before it snapped like a slingshot and sent Curt flying back in the direction he came from. Gracey realized too late that she was right in Curt's path. Curt knocked her onto her rear end as he flew past her and landed, with a thud, on the ground. Their peg legs were lying ripped on the ground next to them.

Cuddles watched Curt fly away from him and chuckled. He looked a bit bored as he flicked one of his sharp claws out to inspect it.

"This looks like fun," he said, watching with amusement. "Snakes and spiders make tasty treats."

The sunlight glinted on his teeth as his mouth spread into another evil grin.

Gracey managed to get back on her feet first. She saw that Cuddles was getting ready to pounce while Alvin and Thaddeus were both still frozen in terror on the spot.

"Thaddeus! Alvin!" she commanded. "Divide and retreat!"

They didn't move.

"Now!" she screamed.

Both the snake and the little spider jumped in surprise at the sound of her voice. They leapt in opposite directions. Cuddles dropped his sharp claws on the same spot where they had just been standing.

Cuddles looked under his paw, bewildered, and then looked around. Alvin and Thaddeus raced back to where Gracey and Curt were now hiding in a hole under the corner of the shed.

Thaddeus was trying so hard to run fast that his legs got tangled up together and he stumbled. His peg leg shredded and he tripped on it as he tried to run.

"Thaddeus!" Gracey cried.

Alvin looked across at Thaddeus. He saw

Cuddles looking to where the little spider had fallen. Alvin raced over, gently scooped Thaddeus up with his mouth, and raced for the hole. He could hear Cuddles catching up to them. He flicked his tail and his peg tail flew off, distracting Cuddles for just a second. The hole was just ahead. Just as they reached the entrance, Alvin tossed Thaddeus in and then slithered in after him. Cuddles poked his paw into the hole, but he couldn't stretch far enough.

Inside, Thaddeus stared in horror as the cat's extended claws came dangerously close to him. Curt pulled him back and the four of them retreated just out of Cuddles's reach.

"Sorry I threw you," Alvin apologized to Thaddeus.

"That's OK," Thaddeus replied in relief. "Really. Thanks for coming back for me!"

"Anytime," Alvin smiled at his new friend.

Cuddles peered in the hole, his face filling the opening.

"Now I have you!"

"We need to do something!" Gracey whispered.

Cuddles leaned further into the hole and his claw nearly touched Alvin. The snake squeezed back as far as he could.

"What do we do?" Curt whispered back.

"I'm thinking!" Gracey answered.

"Well, think a little faster!" he replied.

Just then Alvin poked his head against the side wall of the hole, and it gave way. This side was made of leaves and not dirt.

"I have an idea if we can get out of here first," said Thaddeus.

Alvin held his breath and pushed through the other side of the hole. Daylight streamed in.

"Well, that worked. Thanks Alvin!" said Curt, astonished.

"Wow, thanks Alvin!" Gracey added as she climbed out of the hole.

All four were out of the hole while Cuddles was still reaching blindly with his claws through the front entrance.

"What's your idea?" Alvin asked Thaddeus.

"Well," Thaddeus knew his idea wasn't going to be very popular. "Curt, I need you to distract Cuddles."

"You need me to what?" Curt practically squealed.

Thaddeus pointed to a long branch sticking out from the nearby woodpile.

"Gracey, you need to spin a long stretchy web and a long strong web and twist them together," Thaddeus began. "Curt, you're going to hang from that branch like a cat toy – like those ones with the feather on the stick – and bounce around a lot to distract Cuddles."

"A cat toy? You want me to be a cat toy? That's your plan, Thaddeus?" Curt couldn't believe what he was hearing.

"I'm very serious!" Thaddeus replied. "You and Alvin are going to distract him while Gracey and I get the cannons ready."

"Cannons?" Gracey asked in astonishment.

The three looked at Thaddeus like they hadn't quite heard correctly. But Thaddeus was totally in control of the situation, "You'll see! Now let's get moving!"

The command in Thaddeus's voice made Gracey, Curt, and Alvin snap to attention.

Spider Fact: Spiders are Arachnids and are distant cousins to scorpions, mites, and ticks.

Chapter 8

Ready, Aim, Fire!

Under Thaddeus's supervision, the four tackled their assigned tasks. It would take a lot of hard work to make this plan take shape.

To assemble the cat toy, Curt and Alvin strung a long line of Gracey's web from the branch sticking out of the woodpile. It kind of looked like a fishing rod. They attached the other end to Curt's harness along with the feather from his pirate hat. Alvin wanted to make sure Curt really looked like a cat toy. Once Alvin boosted him up to the stick, Curt crawled the rest of the way up to the far end of the stick and tucked away out of sight.

Cuddles was still blindly trying to find them in the hole as Alvin quietly moved into position across from Curt.

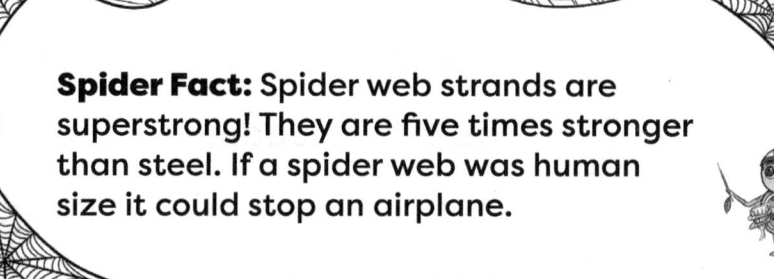

Spider Fact: Spider web strands are superstrong! They are five times stronger than steel. If a spider web was human size it could stop an airplane.

"Here, kitty-kitty!" Alvin called out.

Cuddles stopped digging in the hole and looked around. He spotted Alvin, standing almost on his tail, dancing back and forth like a cobra. Curt, watching from his hiding spot on the end of the stick, was seriously impressed. To the shock of both Curt and Cuddles, Alvin began break dancing. He spun dizzyingly fast on his head and then leapt high in the air and did a complete backflip.

Whoa, thought Curt. *That is outrageously cool!*

Cuddles was less impressed but Alvin's moves made him irresistible to the cat's feline sensibilities. Cuddles pounced, but Alvin saw him coming and dodged out of the way, just in time. Cuddles spun around, confused, searching for his prey.

That was Curt's cue. He let go of the stick and bounced down. Suspended by the web, he looked exactly like a tiny cat toy on a stick.

"Hey Cuddles," he called out as he swung in circles.

Like an acrobat, Curt bounced, bobbed, and spun in elaborate circles to distract Cuddles. It worked! Cuddles started batting at Curt, his claws coming dangerously close. Curt, however, was a natural acrobat and could bust some moves of his own.

While Cuddles was distracted Alvin moved to another location and started showing off some more of his dance wizardry.

"Come and get me!" Alvin called out to Cuddles.

Cuddles took the bait and pounced in Alvin's direction, abandoning Curt. He missed again.

While Alvin and Curt continued their tag

team distraction plan, Thaddeus and Gracey were busy making cannonballs. A large pile of balls fashioned out of a gooey combination of mud, slug slime, and tiny rocks had already been assembled and Thaddeus and Gracey were in peak production mode. They were each grabbing piles of mud, slug slime, and the little rocks and then juggling them with several legs to fashion them into dense balls. Their legs were flying at a dazzling speed and the pile of cannonballs was growing fast.

Without even looking, Thaddeus reached for another pile of mud. He had started juggling when it suddenly wriggled and yelled. It was a pill bug and it wasn't very happy. The bug unrolled itself just as Thaddeus caught it.

"Hey!" the pill bug exclaimed. "Watch it!"

"Oops, sorry!" Thaddeus apologized as he gently put the annoyed bug down on the ground where it stomped away indignantly.

Gracey looked over at Curt and Alvin. She could see they were getting tired and Curt's web was starting to fray.

"Thaddeus," she said, "we have to do this."

"You're right," he agreed. "Just one more."

Thaddeus gathered a pile of thorns from a nearby rosebush and brought them over.

"Noooo," Gracey shuddered. "We can't."

"We might have to," Thaddeus said grimly. "It's our last resort." He didn't like it any more than she did but he knew they might not have any other choice.

They rolled a large ball, three times the size of the other cannonballs, and carefully added rose thorns around the outside with some sticky webbing. This was a seriously deadly weapon!

Gracey and Thaddeus looked at the sharp thorns. There were a lot of them.

"We can't," Gracey said. "That many thorns could really hurt him."

"He's going to hurt us!" Thaddeus exclaimed.

"I know, but if we really hurt him then we are just as mean as him. There needs to be another way," she pleaded.

Thaddeus thought about that and he had to agree.

"Look," she compromised, "we just want him to run away so we can escape. Why don't we take out a bunch of the thorns so that if any side hits him, it will only be one thorn that sticks, not a bunch. That way we aren't going to permanently injure him."

"OK," Thaddeus agreed reluctantly. "But our aim is going to have to be perfect. If we miss by even a little, less thorns means less chance of distracting him."

"Thaddeus, we will have perfect aim. I know it!" Gracey said, relieved.

"Alvin!" Thaddeus called as Curt kept Cuddles distracted. "Over here!"

Alvin raced over as fast as he could. There was no time to lose.

"Can you make a coil? About this wide?" Gracey asked him, drawing a reference example so he could see exactly what to do.

Alvin saw right away what the plan was. He quickly formed himself into a spring-like coil. While Gracey masterfully wove a web around one of the coils to make a slingshot, Thaddeus removed most of the thorns from the thorn cannonball, leaving one for every width of Cuddles's nose. The cannonballs would be directed through the coils and launched toward their target – Cuddles.

Gracey and Thaddeus placed three of the smaller balls onto the slingshot and pulled it back as hard as they could, anchoring themselves on Alvin's tail. Alvin closed one of his eyes to sharpen his aim. Gracey and Thaddeus were shaking from the strain of pulling on the web.

"Hurry up!" Curt called as one of Cuddles's claws nearly caught him.

"Fire!" Gracey yelled.

They let go and the cannonballs flew through the air, startling Cuddles as they hit him on the side of the head. Cuddles wiped the slime off his fur.

"Slug slime?" Cuddles sneered. "That's the best you've got?"

"Yoo-hoo!" Curt sang as he swung right in

front of Cuddles's eyes. Cuddles absolutely could not resist a good cat toy.

A steady stream of cannonballs pummeled Cuddles as he focused his attention on Curt. He was covered in slime and mud but all he cared about was catching that spider!

"It's not working!" Gracey cried as they sent the last of their slug slime and mud cannonballs toward Cuddles.

"We have no choice," said Thaddeus. "We have to use the thorn ball."

Thaddeus, Gracey, and Alvin looked at the large ball with the sharp thorns. It was bigger and meaner than all the others but they had no choice.

"Line it up to hit him on the nose," Gracey told Alvin. "If we miss it won't work." Alvin nodded; it was the only way.

Gracey and Thaddeus rolled the ball onto the slingshot. It was very heavy and hard to roll but they were determined. Curt's web was fraying, and they knew he couldn't hold out much longer.

"This is going to hurt," Thaddeus grunted as they moved the ball into position.

"I don't think it will do any permanent

damage," said Gracey.

"If he was in a bad mood before," Alvin said grimly, "this definitely isn't going to make it any better."

The others nodded in solemn agreement.

Curt was exhausted. Cuddles was getting closer every time he swung his paws.

The cannon, made with Alvin's coils, was in position. Gracey and Thaddeus were straining at the extra weight of the huge and very deadly cannonball. Alvin looked determined as he carefully focused his aim.

"I can't hold on much longer!" Curt called desperately.

"Ready?" Thaddeus commanded.

"Ready!" Gracey answered, her legs ready to give out.

"Aim?" Thaddeus said to Alvin.

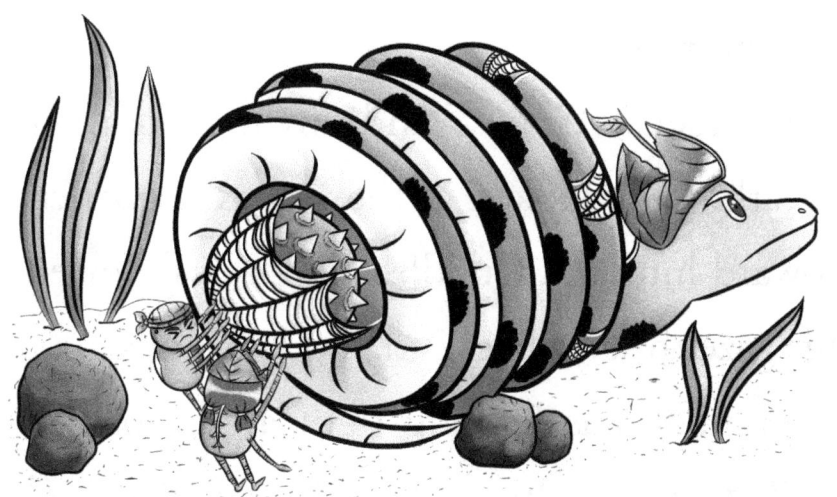

"Aiming!" Alvin replied, more focused than he had ever been. His muscles shifted slightly as he fine-tuned his positioning.

"Fire!" Thaddeus yelled.

Thaddeus and Gracey let go and the deadly thorn ball flew up the tunnel of Alvin's coils and off into the air. The two spiders fell onto the ground and then scrambled up to watch the ball's progress.

"Come on," Thaddeus whispered, willing it to reach its target. Cuddles was moving around too much.

Thaddeus, Gracey, and Alvin held their breath. Curt looked at the ball as it hurtled toward him and Cuddles. Cuddles followed his gaze to see what Curt was looking at.

Cuddles was looking right at the ball as it flew toward his nose. His eyes widened when he realized what was happening. But it was too late!

The thorn cannonball hit Cuddles square in the nose, right on target.

Cuddles screamed in pain as the ball stuck to the soft fleshy part of his nose. He batted it away but one of the thorns was firmly attached. He ran in circles, trying to dislodge the thorn but he was only pushing it in further.

"I'll get you pirates!" he cried as he ran into the house. "This isn't over!"

Just as Cuddles disappeared into the house Curt's web finally broke. He hit the ground with a thud – something he had done many times that day already.

"Ow!" he grunted as he looked up into the worried faces of Gracey, Thaddeus, and Alvin who had all raced over to help him.

"Great job, Curt!" Thaddeus said enthusiastically. "Let's go find this snake pit so we can make it home before dinner. I'm getting hungry."

"Super," Curt muttered under his breath as he laid on the ground, exhausted, while his fellow pirates walked away. "More snakes!"

Chapter 9

Smooth Sailing

Once again Gracey and Curt were soaring high above the garden while Alvin and Thaddeus led the way down below. Gracey held on tightly to the harness but she was almost OK with looking down. They were all happy, a little tired, and a little hungry. Actually, they were a lot tired and a lot hungry!

After they handled the Cuddles problem it

was smooth sailing for the rest of the journey to Alvin's house.

Spider Fact: Spiders don't have wings but they can fly across oceans on strands of webbing.

Alvin and his family lived in a deep hole surrounded by grass and rocks at the end of the garden. The hole faced out from a slight hill where the family enjoyed a lovely view and the rocks provided plenty of places for Alvin and his many brothers and sisters to hide and play.

Gracey was the first to spot the hole after they left the garden shed.

"I see it!" she yelled excitedly. "Alvin, turn ten degrees to port and it will take us straight there."

Alvin adjusted his course according to Gracey's directions and increased his speed. As they neared the hole Gracey could just see tiny green heads poking up from between the rocks. There were dozens of them.

Curt could also see them. Although he and Alvin had become excellent friends, his fear of snakes was still there, gurgling deep inside him. It would take some time for him to work it out. He was alarmed at the sight of all those little heads, but he took a deep breath, put on his biggest smile, and faced his fears.

"Alvin," Curt asked out of curiosity. "Exactly how many brothers and sisters do you have?"

"Seventy-one including me!" he beamed proudly. "I'm the oldest!" Alvin's heart was very happy as he had spotted his brothers and sisters now too.

Alvin came to a gentle stop and Curt and Gracey came to a soft landing on the grass. Curt was pretty sure it was the first soft landing he'd had all day. Alvin lowered his head and Thaddeus slid down his neck and onto the grass where Curt and Gracey were already waiting.

Alvin was swarmed by his many little brothers and sisters.

"Alvin, you're back!" squealed the little snakes in excitement. "Where did you get that awesome pirate hat?" they were all asking, obviously jealous of their older brother's exceptional pirate accessory.

"My new friends made it!" he exclaimed, proudly. "This is Gracey, Thaddeus, and that's Curt."

The three spiders waved their multiple legs. "The hat," he added, "was Gracey's design. She made me a peg tail too but I sort of lost it."

Instantly Gracey was surrounded by more little snakes than she could count. "Can we get pirate hats and peg tails too?" they begged.

"Uh, sure," she laughed. "I think I

can do that."

Just then, Alvin's mom, Susannah, slithered out of the hole. She was very tall… if a snake could be called tall. Or was she long? No matter. She had a huge, warm smile, horn-rimmed glasses, and a very neat ponytail. She was wearing a white lab coat.

"Alvin, dear. Who are your new friends?" she asked.

"Hi Mom! This is Gracey, Thaddeus, and Curt," he announced, pointing to each of the little spiders as he introduced them. "They helped me get home. I got lost," he continued. "The grass was too deep after the rain." He smiled sheepishly.

"This is my mom," he said to his three new spider friends. "She's a scientist!"

"Cool!" said Thaddeus, in awe. "I'm pleased to meet you, Mrs....?" He realized he didn't know Alvin's last name.

"Adderly, Thaddeus. And I'm very pleased to meet you as well." She nodded at him. "My name is Dr. Susannah Adderly and it's nice to meet all of you. Thank you all for helping my Alvin get home!"

"It was our pleasure, Dr. Adderly," Gracey said.

"Hey," Thaddeus said solemnly to Gracey and Curt. "I just realized. We still need to get home. It's a long way. We need to get going or we'll never make it." Curt and Gracey knew Thaddeus was right.

"Um," Alvin interrupted. "I have an idea."

Chapter 10

Flying Spiders

For the second time that day, Alvin's coils were set up in what was now being referred to as the cannon formation. All of his brothers and sisters, each sporting a new pirate hat and peg tail, were positively squirming with excitement.

Gracey, Thaddeus, and Curt stood back and appraised the contraption. It had been a group effort between all of the snakes and the spiders. Math calculations were done by Dr. Adderly (and approved by Thaddeus). Gracey spun the webs. Curt offered unwanted opinions on why everything needed to go faster. Alvin's exceptional muscular control was the final piece of the plan to get the little spiders home before dinner.

Once everything was set up, however, Gracey was not quite so confident. She looked at the contraption with a bit of concern and then looked nervously into the distance toward their home.

"So, we're the cannonballs?! Is this safe?" Gracey asked.

"Yes, I guess you are the cannonballs, and of course, it's perfectly safe!" Dr. Adderly moved around Alvin's coils, double-checking her calculations.

"Alright," Alvin's mother said, "Gracey, let's have you go first."

"Why me?" Gracey asked, alarmed. "Why not Curt?"

"Because," Dr. Adderly replied, "you are the tallest and this will give the kids here a good sense of how hard they need to pull for Thaddeus and Curt."

"But Curt actually *likes* flying, and he likes heights, and he gets injured all the time. He's used to it!"

"It's all just science, Gracey," Thaddeus said as if it made total sense.

That makes absolutely no sense! Gracey thought to herself but was careful not to say it aloud. Thaddeus and Curt, however, were nodding sagely in agreement. Gracey was sure they were both trying hard not to laugh.

Gracey now resembled a parachute, with a band of webbing and a leaf between each of her legs on both sides. She could walk with some difficulty, but when she spread  out her legs, she looked like a round bat or maybe a tiny flying squirrel. She managed to shuffle over and crawl onto the superstrong web platform she had woven between Alvin's coils. At least that part of the device she was confident in. She really was the best web spinner at school.

Gracey positioned herself and pulled her helmet down as tightly as she could. Dr. Adderly gave her some last-minute instructions.

"Now remember, Gracey," she explained, "when you are flying keep your legs straight back and make yourself into the shape of a snake – long and thin. When you are approaching your yard, spread your legs wide and you will float down gently like a parachute! If all goes well," she added, "you should have very good control as you land. And that's it. You're ready to go!"

"That's it?" Gracey burst out.

Dr. Adderly looked puzzled, "Do you have any questions?"

Gracey gulped and shook her head. She could think of lots of stories where parachutes crashed but decided not to mention them.

Dr. Adderly stepped back from the launch area.

"Ready?" she commanded.

All the little snakes snapped to attention and grabbed the handles that had been woven into the back of the sling. Gracey closed her eyes and held her breath.

"Arrr!" The replied in unison.

"Set?" Dr. Adderly continued.

The snakes all anchored themselves on Alvin's tail. As one they pulled together, stretching the sling far back into the spring-shaped coil.

Gracey felt the sling lurch backwards and the tension tighten in the webbing she was sitting on. She gulped.

"Fire!"

"Arrr!!!!" The snakes cried together as they let go of the sling. Gracey shot through the tunnel and was launched into the air.

"Aaaaaaaaa," Gracey could be heard screaming until she disappeared into the distance.

"Aaaarrrrrr!" they cried in glee.

Thaddeus and Dr. Adderly watched Gracey as she flew off and double-checked their calculations.

"Perfect angle," Dr. Adderly said approvingly at the disappearing speck that was Gracey.

"Excellent launch, Dr. Adderly," Thaddeus agreed.

"Now," Dr. Adderly said as she looked at Thaddeus. "We'll do you next."

With complete faith in his math and Gracey's web, Thaddeus didn't hesitate to climb onto the sling. It was hard to walk in the parachute suit, but he finally lined himself up next to Alvin's coils and then Dr. Adderly gave him a boost up to the sling. Thaddeus adjusted his helmet.

"Thanks, Dr. Adderly," he grinned. "It was wonderful to meet you!"

"You too, Thaddeus," she smiled. "Come back again and I'll give you a tour of my lab."

"Wow! I would love that! I'll definitely be back," he promised.

Curt rolled his eyes – all of them.

Seconds later, Thaddeus was a tiny dot in the distance.

"Well," Dr. Adderly said looking at Curt. "I guess it's your turn."

Curt couldn't wait. He expertly moved his parachute suit and hopped up on the sling.

"Thanks for everything," he grinned. "And can Alvin come to our house and play some time?"

"Yeah, Mom, can I?" Alvin begged.

"Of course!" Dr. Adderly replied. "And we would love to have you three over as well!" Curt and Alvin, the unlikeliest of friends, grinned at each other.

Curt suspected he was starting to get over his fear of snakes. He was pretty sure he might even like them.

"Now, Curt." Dr. Adderly warned. "Remember the goal here is distance and not speed!"

"Right!" Curt said, as he immediately tucked himself into the speediest position possible.

Dr. Adderly rolled her eyes, which was easier than rolling the eight that Martha had to roll. Curt, she could tell, was all about speed.

Let's hope he doesn't break too many legs, she thought to herself.

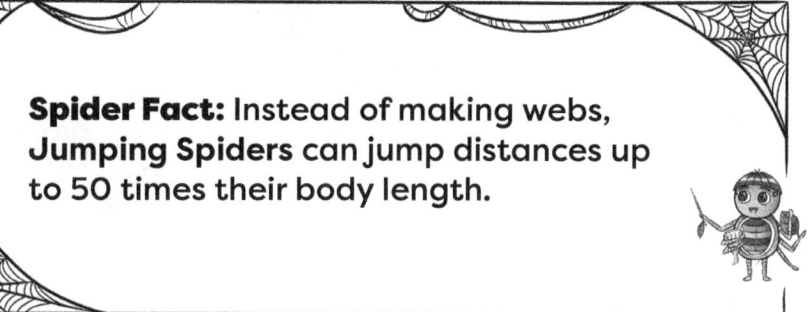

Spider Fact: Instead of making webs, **Jumping Spiders** can jump distances up to 50 times their body length.

Chapter 11

Landing

Three little spiders sped through the air, one after the other, legs straight behind them. They looked like little darts. The wind caused by their high speed pulled the grins back on their faces. As Gracey and Thaddeus saw their yard fast approaching their grins turned to looks of panic. Gracey, first in line, pushed against the wind to open up her parachute suit. The fabric of webbing and leaves ballooned between all eight legs like a kite. She was barely strong enough to fight against the wind but, at the last minute, she finally managed to spread them apart, allowing the parachute to slow her fall.

Thaddeus opened his parachute-laden legs up much earlier than Gracey, calculating he would be able to slow his speed more and soften his landing. Curt, of course, had no plans to slow down until he absolutely had to.

Meanwhile, in the Spyder family kitchen, Martha was idly stirring a yummy pot of fruit fly stew with one of her legs. Tiny fruit fly wings, as well as plenty of herbs and spices were spinning in the broth as her stirring created a whirlpool in the middle of the pot. Two more of her legs were chopping vegetables for the stew. Most of her attention was on the copy of *Modern Spyder Magazine* that had just arrived in the mail. There was a fascinating article about the latest in night-vision goggles.

Martha glanced out the kitchen window. It overlooked their garden, and the sunlight was streaming through the trees. *It looks so peaceful,* she thought.

She had just reached a spoon to her mouth to test the stew when she heard a high-speed screeching noise coming from the yard. Without even lowering the spoon she looked out the window again. She was just in time to see Gracey hurtling out of the sky with some sort of parachute attached to her legs.

"Aaaaaa," she heard Gracey yelling as she landed with a gentle thump.

"Well," Martha said to herself, "that was unexpected. If that was the first," she wondered, "where are the other two?"

She looked again and saw, to her astonishment, Thaddeus, with a similar parachute contraption to Gracey's, carefully floating down to the ground.

Nice landing! Martha thought, *I'm impressed! Now,* she looked up again, *what about number three?*

"Wahoooo!" Curt's unmistakeable howl could be heard from far off in the distance.

Ah, thought Martha. *That's him.*

She watched as Curt backpedalled and activated his parachute a fraction too late. He slowed down a little but landed with a hard bump and a few rolls. He sat up right next to his brother and sister.

"That was awesome!" Curt grinned. "I can see where we can make some improvements to the suits for next time!"

"Next time?!!! Gracey and Thaddeus groaned at the same time. They couldn't believe he just said that.

Inside the kitchen Martha plopped the spoonful of stew into her mouth. "Mmmm," she whispered. "Needs some salt."

Spider Fact: Spiders are good to have in your garden. They eat fruit flies, regular flies, and even mosquitos.

Chapter 12

Spiders Grounded

Later, Martha and all three of the Spyder kids were sitting at the dinner table enjoying hearty bowls of fruit fly stew.

"Where's Dad again?" Gracey asked between mouthfuls.

"He's on a secret mission," answered her mother.

"But where?" asked Curt.

"Well, if I told you it wouldn't be a secret

mission anymore, would it?" She grinned at Curt. "He sent you each a web message you can read after dinner. He said he'll be home for the weekend."

Martha looked around at her three children. *Which*, she thought to herself, *will be the first to crack?*

"So," she asked them, "what did you three do today?"

Gracey, Curt, and Thaddeus looked at each other conspiratorially.

"Nothing much," Curt finally replied. "We just played pirates."

Martha waited to see if any more information was coming. Nothing.

"Thaddeus?" she said.

"Don't do it," Curt whispered under his breath.

But Thaddeus couldn't help it. He had no way to resist the power of Martha's mom stare.

Desperate, he shoved as much stew in his mouth as he could. His cheeks bulged but he still kept shoving more food in. He looked at his mom with an innocent smile. It would be rude to talk with his mouth full.

She looked back at him with an "I can wait you out" look.

Thaddeus eventually gulped the food down. Gracey and Curt were glaring at him.

Avoiding Martha's gaze by looking at the ceiling, he said, "That was delicious, Mom! Dessert?"

Martha laughed and picked up the bowls. Curt reached over and grabbed her issue of *Modern Spyder Magazine*, just in case they got sent to their room.

"That's OK," she said, "Susannah Adderly called and told me everything." She looked pointedly at Thaddeus, who cringed. The three little spiders looked at each other in shock. Their mom was a better spy than they thought.

"And no," their mother continued, "there will be no dessert. There will be, however, extra chores, no TV, and you're definitely grounded for going near the water when I told you not to. But you may receive a *slightly* reduced sentence for helping your friend when he needed it. I'm very proud of all of you for doing that."

She smiled at them with her best triumphant mom smile.

Spider Fact: There are over 2,800 species of **Orb-Weaver Spiders** in the world. They are the spiders most commonly seen in North America. They create webs that extend out from a circular centre.

About the Author

Vesta L. Giles is a writer, filmmaker, and has worked in libraries for many years. She loves listening to audiobooks and hiking, biking, running, and cross country skiing near her home in Kamloops, BC, Canada. Her favourite book when she was growing up was *A Wrinkle in Time* by Madeleine L'engle. Learn more about Vesta and the Spyders at www.vandelsopress.com.

About the Illustrator

Rebecca McKerchar is a digital illustrator based in Kamloops, BC. She received her BFA from Thompson Rivers University, where her studies focused primarily on painting, sculpture, and printmaking. Rebecca has pursued digital art for over ten years now, but considers herself something of a jack-of-all-trades, having dabbled in sewing, textiles, and woodworking alongside her other artistic pursuits. Rebecca's digital art style seeks to combine stark line-art with the painting techniques she developed during university to create vibrant scenes and characters.

Acknowledgements

So much gratitude ...

Thanks to Erin Linn McMullan (Fresh Horses) for her fine editor's eye and for championing *The Spyders*.

Shelly McKerchar is a talented artist who brought the early vision of what the spiders could look like to life. When I decided to turn these stories into books, Shelly suggested her daughter, Rebecca McKerchar, would be perfect…and she is! Rebecca created lively illustrations that are better than I could have imagined.

Putting all of these pieces together with the cover design and layout was Kristina Benson of Dansk Design Group along with Justin Frudd who did the ebook formatting. Great layout is the unsung hero of any book. Together they have made something really special.

— *Vesta*

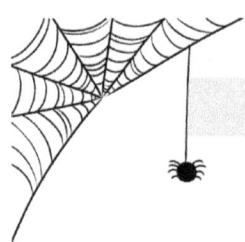

BOOK #2

Keep reading

for a sneak peak at

The Spyders:

Take Your Kids to Work,

the next book in the

Spyders series!

Itinerary

Welcome to Spy School

Your instructors:
    Harold Spyder (also known as "Agent Dad")
    Martha Spyder (also known as "Agent Mom")

Day 1:
- **0600** **Morning**
  Physical Agility Level 1
      Obstacle Course and Strength Training
  Martial Arts
      Jujitsu Level 1
  Teamwork Drills
  Physical Endurance
- **0800** **Breakfast**
- **0900** **Morning (part II)**
  Science:
      Physics, Aerodynamics, Engineering
- **1200** **Lunch**
- **1300** **Afternoon**
  Maps and Navigation

Day 2:
- **0600** **Morning**
  Physical Agility Level 2
      Obstacle Course and Dodgeball
  Martial Arts
      Karate Level 1
  Teamwork Drills
  Physical Endurance
- **0800** **Breakfast**
- **0900** **Morning (part II)**
  Communications:
      Morse Code, Hand and Leg Signals, Web Plucking
- **1200** **Lunch**
- **1300** **Afternoon**
  Gadgets and Spy Gear
  Mission Briefing

Don't be late!
Extra laps if you're not on time.
Hugs, Mom

It was early, very early. Curt was sprawled out in his sleeping pod dreaming of exploring the Amazon jungle. Curled up in her own pod slightly below and to the left of Curt's, Gracey was also dreaming. She was sculpting the most impossible, fantastical piece of art made entirely out of glistening webs. Below Gracey, Thaddeus clutched his teddy spider and floated off on clouds that were filled with numbers and mathematical equations.

Suddenly, in the dreams of all three spiders, a loud clamour jerked them out of their slumber. It was a horrible coughing sound like a goose choking on dry peanut butter. The noise was deafening as it bounced off the walls and buzzed every bristly hair on their bodies. It felt like it was coming from all around them. Still half-asleep and disoriented, all three leapt up in their pods, which started swinging and banging against each other.

The noise continued, getting louder. His heart in his throat, Thaddeus didn't know what was happening. He tripped on his blankets and tumbled out of his pod. He fell straight down to the ground below, landing with a thud. It was dark. Stars were spinning in circles around his eyes. He heard a yell and one of Curt's feet hit him squarely in the nose as Curt landed next to him with a loud crash.

"Ow!" Thaddeus cried.

"Help!" Gracey yelled from above.

With no warning the lights came on. Thaddeus and Curt squinted at the brightness. When their eyes could focus, they looked up and there was Gracey, dangling upside down by one leg while her other legs were tangled in her blanket. Thaddeus looked up at his older sister, who looked like a caterpillar stuck in a cocoon with one leg sticking out.

"Goooooood morning, recruits!" came a booming voice from the door.

The voice belonged to their father, Harold, who was looking disturbingly awake with a clipboard in one hand and a whistle around his neck as he greeted them through a megaphone held in another hand. In a third hand, Thaddeus noted, was an air horn. *Ah,* Thaddeus realized, *the sound of a dying goose.*

Harold, with his short spikey hair and goofy grin, looked like a bit like a drill sergeant although the grin made it hard for him to look very scary.

As Gracey escaped from the blanket and lowered herself down to the floor on a hastily spun web, Harold handed each of the kids a piece of paper from his clipboard. They looked at the papers, their sleepy eyes still trying to focus. Along the top it said, "Itinerary".

"Welcome to Spy School!" Harold grinned.

Ten minutes later Curt, Gracey, and Thaddeus, each holding their itinerary, were in their yard staring at the biggest obstacle course they had ever seen. But it was so early even Curt couldn't get excited about it.

Martha, looking as bright and cheery as Harold, blew the whistle that was hanging around her neck.

"Are you ready?" she yelled.

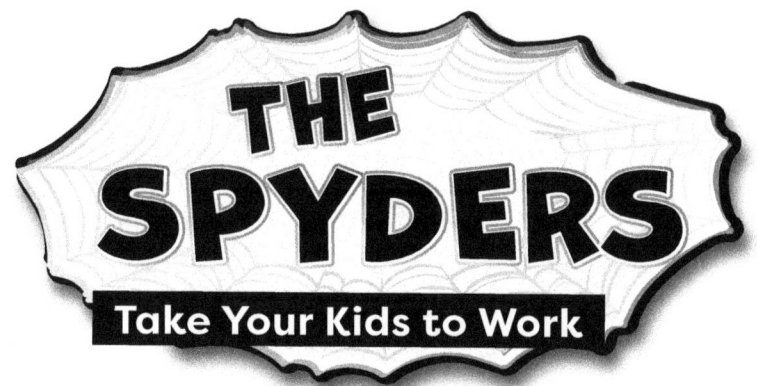

Book 2 in *The Spyders* series,

Coming soon!

What if Curt, Gracey, and Thaddeus went to work for the day with their parents, Martha and Harold, and spent the day being spies? What could possibly go wrong?

For more information on *The Spyders: Take Your Kids to Work* (Book #2 in the series) sign up for our newsletter where you'll find up to date information and occasional freebies!

Find us here for the latest news:

www.vandelsopress.com

Facebook: @vandelsopress
Instagram: @vandelsopress
Twitter: @pressvandelso